Requiem for the Unrequited

Maleeka Mohammed

BookLeaf
Publishing

India | USA | UK

Requiem for the Unrequited © 2024
Maleeka Mohammed

All rights reserved.

Maleeka Mohammed asserts the moral right to be identified as the author of this work.

Presentation by *BookLeaf Publishing*

Web: www.bookleafpub.com

E-mail: info@bookleafpub.com

ISBN: 9789363312883

First edition 2024

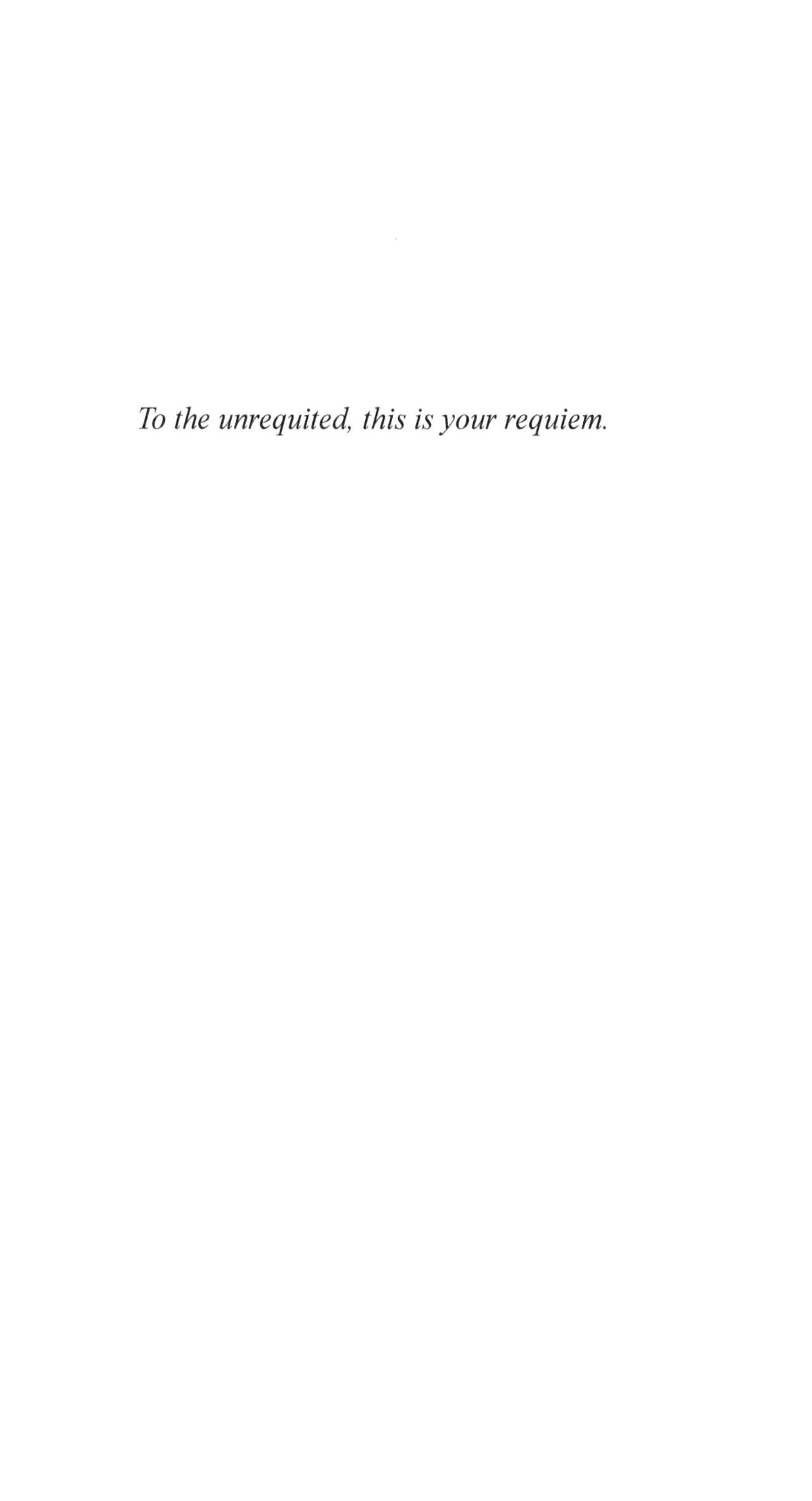

To the unrequited, this is your requiem.

ACKNOWLEDGEMENT

This could not be done without the heartaches. The dark headspace caused by the fake relationships my mind created. Love will always win, but not in this anthology. Love will break you and make you think domestic violence situations are all you are deserving of. There are morbidities to love, and I tried to highlight those within this book. Thank you family, for your support. Lastly, to my favorite demon, your constant encouragement and support never faltered – which helped this creation, thank you.

PREFACE

Reader's discretion is advised. This is not suitable for children. Strong sexual themes and language.

Vocabulary Expansion Course on Requiem of the Unrequited

Reader's discretion is advised.

To think

I am writing this

And it is not even for the preface

But a poem instead.

First!

An English lesson.

More like an opportunity to give a

Vocabulary Expansion Course

Clearly,

Someone

Has a wild imagination

With an artillery of words

Creating new phrases and mottos.

More like mantras

And manifestations.

Breaking down the title into smaller chunks.
Proceed with caution
First word.
Requiem.
Reh
Kwee
Yum...
Yum?

Dear Reader,

If you already know the definition, then you
understand the question.

Requiem
A mass for a dead person.
Seriously Webster?
Dead person?
Couldn't even phrase it better?
With something of sorts as a deceased person,
instead?

Dear Reader,

I'm sorry, but my undiagnosed ADHD is most
definitely illuminated within this piece.

Breaking fourth walls as we traverse through
different dimensions with the gift of knowledge.

Requiem
Back to the dead people.
More like their mass.
Basically,
A funeral
Where we gather at mass for mass
But not finding mass
m= p/v
For my non-STEM readers
Who are reading this
Mass equals density divided by volume.
Imagine!
Being able to measure
The emotional density of a person.
Physical health
Bodily
That density can be measured.
But measure my grief!
Find out how dense
I have become
From gathering
With the masses
For the masses.

Requiem.

A musical service or composition
In honor of the dead.
We honor our dead
Respecting them
As if they are still alive.
Keeping relics
Treasuring artifacts
From eons
That seemed far too long ago.

Mozart.
Wolfgang Amadeus Mozart.
Composer.
This is where
I first heard the word
"Requiem"
An unfinished composition
Due to his death.
Talk about foreshadowing!
Died before
Finishing a musical composition
On death.
Death.
He waits for no one.
Death.
He knows no boundaries.
Mozart,
A musical genius,

Expanding my vocabulary artillery Unknowingly
With a single word
Requiem.
So,
This was the ideology
Behind the "Requiem"
Portion of the title.
Gathering for the funeral.
Memorialization.

Dear Reader,

If you are still reading, thank you for being
patient. We are only halfway through. At least,
for now, it is.

Unrequited.
Un
Ree
Kah
Why
Ted
Where do I start?
Unsure of where the muse came from entirely.
Obviously, my experiences.
~insert some sort of sparkle animation~
[Oh, wait, this is a book!]
But to narrow it down

To save some tears and time.
Oh!
Don't forget the heartache.
Truly impossible at this moment.
I would rather count rice grains from a
10-pound bag
At this point,
Definition.
Apologies; I got sidetracked.
Definition.
I like the vagueness of Webster's.
Not reciprocate or return in kind.

Dear Reader,

For those who know the definition, you must
understand the vagueness previously stated.

Oxford was a bit more eloquent.
Oxford,
He was more eloquent.
Nothing like the rest.
According to Oxford,
(of a feeling, especially love)
Not returned or rewarded.
Being in your presence is a reward in itself.
The emotional reward of reciprocity
Pining away at my neurons

Breaking down the myelin sheaths
And attacking the dendrites.
Neural decomposition.
Would that be just brain-dead?
When I'm around you,
I feel as if I am brain-dead.
Strung up on all types of machinery
To stay alive.
To disconnect from you.
I would be lost
And hurting more.
More than the lack of reciprocity.

Havoc.
[Havoc should have been a word defined
And a muse for a poem.
But not today.
Although I've been writing this for what
Feels like eons.]

Destruction
On my brain
And thoughts
Travel to my heartstrings
Pulling each time there is a pang of
[our new vocabulary word in unison, please]
Unrequited sensations.

Dear Reader,

I apologize for the vocabulary but prepare
yourself for a partial history lesson.

Love
And other emotions of attachments
Are hard to avoid
From the dawn of existence,
Humans
Have always been social creatures.
Gathering in groups.
Migrating the land together.
Evolution
Has granted us
New opportunities
Smarter
[Or so we think]
Abilities to communicate.
Yet feelings
Always
Complicate things.
Complicated complex complicities.

Unrequited.
I sit here before you
Broken.

Grieving
My losses
Those I never won.
The pain
And agony
Of continuity
Repeating
As if this was an
Endless rinse cycle
On a washing machine.
Spinning
Out of control.
Drowning
Spun out again.
More water.
As I think I am able
To breathe again,
Something complicates
My thought process

Overthinking
Overreacting
Overachieving
Overthinking
Overreacting
Overachieving
Overthinking
Overthinking

Overthinking
Overthinking
Underreacting
Overreacting
Overthinking
Overthinking
Overthinking

Dear Reader,

I am not sure if you signed up for a fucked up one-sided love story or maybe a couple that inspired this book. But here it is. Thank you and enjoy.

With love,

St. Inkbrains

One-Sided Ping Pong Tournament

During the quiet,
Still moments of the morning,
Who do you turn to?
For comfort?
For peace?
For love?
I know it isn't me.
Nor will it ever be.

The mind is a cruel entity.
Creating a universe that could never exist.
Nor will they ever be in existence.
Impossible possibilities
But, yet,
During the quiet,
Still moments of the morning
I turned to you.
For comfort.
For peace.
For love.

Magnetism

I did not want things
To go the way that they did.
A sequence of consequences
Spiraling
Out of control.
Leading me deeper into
My internal turmoil.
Emotions unstable.
Hormonal imbalances.
Brain fog.
Misconstrued communications.

Running in circles.
A constant push and pull.
Polar opposites.
Like magnets.
But not really.
Polar opposites
In regards to magnets attract.
Rather than two of the same.
Pushing and sliding off of each other.
Still touching
Yet not fully embracing
We are like magnets.
We are both hurt.
And hurting.

In the rhythm of everything
Broken.
Breaking.
Shattered.
Tired.
Lonely.
We are the same.
Yet you do not want me.
Nor will you ever.

Maybe
Perhaps,
Just maybe
There is some possibility
That you do want me.
However,
I can tell
It is not the same way
That I want you

Again,
With being hurt
And hurting
Broken.
Breaking.
Shattered.
Tired.
Lonely.

We are the same
Yet,
With different intentions.
I am content with being wanted
If it means being around you
I am
Like a magnet
Attracted to you
Your polar opposite.
Unfortunately.
It is what it is.
My internal turmoil eats away at my pancreas.
Knowing that you would never want me
And you do not want me.
Nor will you ever.

Insomnia

In a constant state of sleepiness.
Tired.
Exhausted.
Totally knackered.
Failed attempts to sleep.
You keep me awake.
Haunting my dreams
With your beauty.
Turning peaceful slumbers
Into nightmare induced anxiety attacks

How can I possibly get better?
I cannot sleep
How can I possibly get better if you aren't next
to me?
My nights now
Remain sleepless without you.
How idiotic?
To understand that my sleep depends on you
Which ultimately does not make any sense
To understand that sleep depends on
Another being is delusional
Nevertheless
The nights remain sleepless

Captured

I am held against my will.
No freedom at all.
His words,
Wishes,
Commands.
All before my needs.

I am nothing but a slave.
To companionship.
Traitor to my own self.
Not able to stand on my feet.
No sense of autonomy.
Even through courtship and marriage
I am to stay.
For what reason?
Not love.
Never for love.
Just for sexual acts
Not even sensual.
Only a mere play toy.
For your pleasure and satisfaction.

Forever?

To serve?
I am not bound by emotions
Although my emotions control me.
Heart and brain act on their own accord.
With that being said,
What do I result in doing?
Crawling back to you.
As if my own well-being doesn't matter.
Honestly,
It probably does not.
Thus, why do I stay?
Why do I allow you to abuse and use me?
A captured slave.
A tortured empath.

The Sky

It reminds me of you
The clouds are pink.
Pink is no longer my favorite color.
You wouldn't know that
We don't talk anymore
Yet I am still reminded of you.
I wonder if you still love me
Like the first day
You said those three words
Do you think about me when something
exciting happens?
Or when your mother cooks your favorite dish
for dinner?
I cut you off
I was the one to break out of this confided cell
But you are
Constantly
A prevalent thought
In my mind.

Vice Grip

He holds my head
Fingers intertwining with my hair
He holds my head
And my heart
But I don't know.

He holds my head
Pulling me closer
To force more of his cock
Into my mouth.

He holds my head
And my heart
But he doesn't know.
Nor can I tell him
Not yet, at least.

He holds my head
Telling me words of encouragement
"Take it deeper, baby"
"Deepthroat this cock like I trained you to."
Pushing my head down if need be.
"That's my girl."

He holds my head

And my heart
But he doesn't know.
Nor can I tell him.
Not yet, at least.
Maybe never, honestly.

He holds my head
And my heart
Every time he tugs at my hair
He tugs at my heart
Creating unreciprocated feelings
And shattered glass shards around my mind.
Dictating my headspace
Like I am a puppet.
Or maybe I am just that good at being used?

He holds my head
He holds my heart
He holds everything that keeps me tranquil
He will never be mine.
But I will enjoy those interactions
And continue to bite my tongue.

He holds my head
And I hold his thigh
Like a lost child.
Savoring this moment
As I allow my mind to go blank

Drowning my demons
Or at least I thought so.
But I couldn't
They know how to swim.
They will outlive me
And follow me
Into my next life
As well as the one right after.

He holds my head
And my heart
But he doesn't know
He doesn't know
He doesn't know
He doesn't know

Valley Of Peace and Toxicity

Peace.
Delicate.
He reminds me of lilies of the valley
Small yet so noticeable
Grabbing my attention
With the curved, bell-shaped flowers
Drooping ever so softly.

Peace is delicate
He reminds me of lilies of the valley
They are poisonous
Memories and thoughts of him
Cloud my head
Causing a toxic headspace
Negatively affecting my thought process
Making everything sour.

Peace was delicate
He reminds me of lilies of the valley.
They bloom mid-spring to early summer
When the weather is amazing
And responsibilities seem the least of my
worries

User and Abuser

I have come to realize
My worth is so much more
That he treats me.

I was your solace during lonely
moments in the morning
Forever,
Just a phone call
or a text message away.

Always,
available
for the wrong people
and never myself
Allowing them back in
Continuously
even after the heartbreaks

I am only good enough for
2 o'clock in the morning
drunken phone calls
Begging me
because of the eruption

of your sexual desires
as if I am some common whore
picked off the street
to be fucked for your pleasure
Plans for meeting up
transition to gold-plated shit
like the gilded lies
you speak
whispering sweet nothings
in hopes of getting into my underwear
but the only place you crawled into
was my heart
like an infestation
of wood-eating termites
in the walls of a forgotten home

Why do we believe having a love like this is
beneficial?
as if this is the only type of love
I am capable of having.
But I still think I am undeserving of love
or a relationship
someone to call mine
marriage
to be able to rely on them.

Forever.

Why do I think this?
A girl like me is not
meant to be running around
with hoodlums
and gangsters.
Or even a person who
claims me
as an object for possession.

I have come to realize
my worth
and my value
my time
my energy
and my dedication
is deserving of someone else.
not you.

My mistakes needed to be made
So I can learn from them
Grow from them
and prosper without you.

Thank you for being
a mistake
a lesson
and
one of my loves.

I still love you.
Or at least so I thought.
I loved
the thought of you.
And the idols you spoke of
The philosophy
That you conveyed
But to say that.
That I still love you
It is a mistake.
Months pass by
And
I continue
Making the same
Mistakes
Allowing you my time
My time is precious
And you are not
Nor will you ever be.

I do not regret
Anything we have done
Or my energy
I devoted to you
But please know
Our relationship
Is completely and totally
Unsalvageable

Do not bother me again
You have been blocked.

Pastry Affair

Being in love
is so vague
There is not some
certain model
or structure to follow.
Every love
is different
Like a snowflake
falling and floating
ever so delicately from
the clouds above.
No two patterns are the same.

I sat there
staring at the empty plate
strewn with crumbs
evidence of the massacre
devoured
but so loved.
loved so much to be devoured.
That was my croissant.
Unable to reciprocate the feelings
I killed her.

Comfort

Safe haven
Solace
Ignorance
Oblivious
Fuzzy blankets
Warm socks
Hot chocolate
Oversized sweaters
Enveloping yourself in freshly dried
bedsheets
from the dryer
embracing the heat
like a loving handshake.

How can a handshake be loving?
Why?
Why do I want the days to never end with
you?
Like an icicle on a hot summer day
I don't want you to go
I don't want this to end.

There is nothing between us.

There is everything between us.
But there could be more
blossoming in our garden
we planted together
unknowingly
you planted blueberry bushes
fruitful
our relationship
but the thorns are your walls
your walls, you bring down briefly
and I caught a glimpse of you.
The real you.
That provides
Safe haven
Solace
Ignorance
Oblivion
Fuzzy blankets
My comfort
Yet, also,
My torment

Story of the Year

With all the mishaps
from the year so far
I have given up.
On love and relationships, that is
Devoting my energy,
my time
my peace.
For nothing in return.
To be blindsided.

Freshly soaked by a car
splashing the puddle onto my being.
I am invisible.
Not inevitable
Irrevocably erroneous relationships
Yes!
Emphasis on the plural.
Failure after failure.
The repetitive negative nature of my existence.
Leading me onto a paved path
Straight to self-impending doom.
Dramatic.
That's what it takes to be a Libra.

450

Karma is a bitch
And you and her have a resemblance.
That is what 450 sang
But I couldn't help from
Shaking my head in agreement.

Did I think our forever would end?
No!
Did I think you could have been such a
cruel person?
No!
Do I think we could ever work on the
relationship?
No!

You have changed so much.
Or maybe my perspective has shifted.
It is as if a light
Is illuminating all the flaws
And wrongdoings
You have done in the past.
When I defended you.
Like the saint, I thought you were.

Pristine like an angel.
I wish I could take back
Those things I said.
I know that I broke your trust.
So did you.
And purposely went out of your way
To hurt me
Emotionally and mentally.

Karma is a bitch
and you and her have a resemblance.
That is what 450 sang
but I couldn't help from
shaking my head in agreement.

Memorialized

I lean against the wall of the fountain.
a memorial
for all that we lost
but I lost her...
Forever
I didn't care about the rest that was gone
she was the only thing
and person
important to me
my forever
and now my forever is gone.

Back to this God–Forsaken fountain
Her name carved into the black stone
I trace with my fingers on my right hand
my left hand gripping tightly
onto the engagement ring
She was snatched away from me
Leaving me empty

Puppeteer of Emotions

I think of you when I am happy
I think of you when I am lonely
I think of you when I am sad

Every single thought I have
Leads back to you
You spark every emotion

I think of you when I need cock
I think of you when I need to be filled
I think of you when I desire you physically

When having you in my thoughts isn't
enough
You poison my mind
Clouding everything
Sometimes even my vision

I need you always to be there
And be my puppeteer of emotions

Mood Swings

Hormonal imbalances.
Mood swings
It has become the norm
Talking puts me on edge
and you cause a lot of anger

You don't exactly know
how much anger you cause.
The existential weight
of our relationship
has me ensnared
and it feels like it is
progressively
getting dragged out
hour
by
hour
second
by
second
until I get no release
and
explode.
Are we even a couple?
Or are you delusional
And I'm trying to move on?

Move forward.
Traverse through this scary thing
We call life.
But could I really do it?
By myself is the real question.
We all need someone
Regardless of the constraints of the relationship.
Whether it be
Sexually,
Platonic,
Emotionally,
Spiritually,
Or moral support companionship.
Back to your delusional thinking.
Staying together is more detrimental than apart.
To continue down
This path of destruction
Is basically self harm
At this point.

Garden of Forgotten

The sun
It showers me with warmth
It will be a great day

"Good morning, world"
I exclaimed into the air
Rhetorically, of course!
Surrounded by my neighbors
They also preparing for the new day
It will be a great day

Stretching in synchronization
Shaking off the remnants of last night's
slumber
We stand tall
Greeting all the park-goers and furry
critters
It will be a great day

I do not stand tall
But everyone else does
The lonely jonquil

Encircled by daffodils
Although I am small
It will be a great day

In my previous lives
My soul was tied to other things
In each life
Searching for him
Trying to finally be free
From this curse
When I was able to speak
I never told him
In hopes he would choose me
Without persuasion
He comes to the park
Every afternoon
It will be a great day

Each day, I see him
My hope raises
Sitting there
So stoic
But I know he is hurt
I can feel it

Perks of being an empath
I want to heal him
It will be a great day

He approaches me
Standing tall
Like a lighthouse on the coast
Making me feel inferior
He bends over slightly
And picks one of my neighbors
It will be a great day

It is already the end of April
May will be starting soon.
My end is nearing.
I will continue to enjoy today
It will be a great day.

I get to see him tomorrow
And the day after tomorrow
And then the day after that
Until my end
It will be a great day

The sunshine

It bathes me in warmth.
The comfort it gives is unparalleled
To any emotion or feeling
I have ever had
It will be a great day to be forgotten.

Won't Work

I am at my end.
This relationship
Built on shit and hurt
It isn't breathing and growing.
Stagnant
Like swamp water

We can remain friends
And find our way
Back to each other.
But will we find our way?
Some rubber bands
They stretch
And snap back
As if nothing ever happened.
Or just break!

Your optimism.
I find it comforting
You believe
Things will resolve
On their own
As if

We are living in a fairy tale
In this plane of existence
There isn't any happily ever after.
Not for long, at least
It does not exist
In this lifetime.

Happily ever after.
It used to be the trend
Living like a princess.
Finding her prince.
Residing in a secluded castle tower
Tucked away from society
Hidden behind mountains and a forest.
That was a dream
From a nightmare
So far in the past
The only beaming light
In the neverending darkness.

But I am at my end
This relationship
It won't work.
It was built on gilded bullshit,
Sex,

Lies,
Hurt
Immoral pleasure seeking.